THE YELLOW HOUSE AT ARLES
Gauguin / van Gogh

by Dennis Hayes
and Richard Payne

PLAYWRIGHTS CANADA

THE YELLOW HOUSE AT ARLES
Gauguin/van Gogh

PLAYWRIGHTS CANADA is the imprint of PLAYWRIGHTS UNION OF CANADA.

PLAYWRIGHTS UNION OF CANADA
8 York Street, 6th Floor
Toronto, Ontario
Canada M5J 1R2
Phone (416) 947-0201

PLAYWRIGHTS UNION OF CANADA operates with generous assistance from
the Canada Council, the Ontario Ministry of Citizenship and Culture,
the Ontario Arts Council, Alberta Culture, Wintario, Metropolitan
Toronto, and the City of Toronto through the Toronto Arts Council.

Cover graphic by Richard Payne
Back cover photo by Andrew Oxenham
Cover design by Jenny Cheng-Burke
Editor: Ann Jansen

ISBN 0-88754-375-8

First Edition: October 1984

Printed and bound in Canada

The authors gratefully acknowledge funding assistance from the
Canada Council and the Ontario Arts Council.

This play is dedicated in memory of

Suzanne Elizabeth Payne (1953-1983),

a sister artist. And to

David Katulski,

our brother in the work.

THE YELLOW HOUSE AT ARLES was first presented as an extended one-act play at Harbourfront Theatre, Toronto, in February 1978. This full-length version was first presented at Tarragon Theatre, Toronto, in January 1983, with the following cast:

PAUL Gauguin . . . . . . Dennis Hayes

VINCENT van Gogh . . . . Richard Payne

Directed by Frank Canino

Set, Costumes and Lighting designed by
Phillip Silver

Paintings created by Richard Payne

Soundscape composed and performed by Allen Booth

Stage Management by Robert Fox

Consulting Dramaturge, Urjo Kareda

Obligatory Programme Notes and Credits:

October to Christmas, 1888
Arles, in Provence.

"The essentials for life are water and bread, and
clothing, and a house, to cover one's nakedness."
(Sirach 29: 21-22)

THE YELLOW HOUSE AT ARLES was first presented by
Tarragon Theatre, Toronto, in January 1983;
dramaturgy by Frank Canino and Urjo Kareda;
assisted in development by Chris Hallgren and
Brian Shein; directed by Frank Canino. The
authors are members of Playwrights Union
of Canada.

The playscript for this and other plays by the
authors are available through Playwrights Union
of Canada, 8 York Street, 6th Floor, Toronto,
Ontario M5J 1R2; tel (416) 947-0201.

Authors' Notes:

THE YELLOW HOUSE AT ARLES is a two-man show in a
single setting. Paul Gauguin and Vincent van Gogh,
two of the founders of Modern Art, spent two months
living and working together in isolation in the
South of France; their intent was to create a
school of new painting which would bring
commercial success for themselves and their fellow
artists.

The play deals with the impact of poverty, the art
market, and technology on the artist, both as
craftsman and as human being. It speaks to basic

human needs -- family, recognition, vision --
and the love and affirmation of another person.

These two "giants" were, after all, living,
ordinary human beings -- two guys who thought
they could work together, but couldn't.

Staging:

A spare, semi-open space generally suggests the
ground floor of the Yellow House. Rudimentary
elements define an area where kitchen and studio
co-exist, centred on a table and the two artists'
chairs (as depicted in van Gogh's canvases).

The upstage area allows paintings to be stacked
or hung; the downstage area is completely open,
to allow for working outdoors; GAUGUIN begins
and ends the play in an isolated area to one side.
The borders of these specific areas are indeter-
minate; locale is defined in the playing and by
the lighting.

The main properties, indicated in the script, are
kitchen and artists' supplies. Costume demands
are minimal: a basic indoor outfit for each
character, with hats and coats for outdoor scenes.
The actors need perform only rudimentary sketching
or carving; dry brush is used during scenes
where painting is part of the action.

Artworks essential to the play's action are
indicated in the script, though others may be
integrated as desired. These are "original
adaptations" of documented works, and the
authors stipulate that no commercial print
reproductions may be used: all carvings,
drawings and paintings must be built with real

materials to a level of reasonable facsimile.
Each work depicted must incorporate clearly trans-
lated aspects: a new colour scheme, shift in
perspective, change in size/proportion/medium,
reduction of descriptive elements -- or appearance
as a work-in-progress. (The artworks required are
available for rental from the authors.)

The soundscape scored for the first production
provides transition during blackouts, specific
environments (e.g. the Mistral wind), and
character/mood themes at strategic points in the
play's action. Flexibility in performance is
achieved by live mixing by the Stage Manager of
two reels of synthesized music (also available
for rental, from the composer, c/o the authors).

ACT ONE: The Building of a Dream

Pre-show: (optional)
Scene One: The Arrival
Scene Two: Breaking Away
Scene Three: Working Together
Scene Four: Candle Hat
Scene Five: Trapped Indoors
Scene Six: Money

ACT TWO: The Experience of Falling Apart

Scene One: The Sulk
Scene Two: Paul Alone
Scene Three: Falling Apart
Scene Four: Vincent Alone
Scene Five: Madmen
Scene Six   Packing Up
Scene Seven: All-night Drunk
Scene Eight: Break-through
Scene Nine: The End

THE YELLOW HOUSE AT ARLES
Gauguin / van Gogh

<u>Act One, Pre-show (Optional)</u>

When the audience enters, the
two actors are working onstage,
in character, but drawing no
attention to themselves.
They are in work-light.

PAUL, in an isolated "island"
away from the Yellow House
interior, is cutting away at
a large wooden sculpture.

VINCENT is engrossed in a
volatile painting, in the
Yellow House.

Both may be smoking pipes.
Both consume a large quantity
of wine, without getting drunk.

They work in silence.

Lights fade to black as play
begins.

<u>Act One, Scene One</u>

THE ARRIVAL

PAUL is packed, and
dressed to travel.

PAUL: How time changes in a journey by rail.
Too fast, not natural. By foot, by
horse, by sail -- you're on the same
time, the traveller and the carrier.
But by rail...! Damned train travels
in a different time than we do, in a
different world. See the landscape --
differently.

         (PAUL arrives at the Yellow House.
         He enters and stands in the
         doorway. VINCENT is slumped in
         sleep at the table. For a
         moment, PAUL takes in VINCENT,
         the painting, the general
         disorder. He makes a decision,
         and rouses VINCENT with a blast
         of a hunting horn. VINCENT
         awakens with a start, disoriented.
         PAUL moves to VINCENT and
         enthusiastically embraces him.
         VINCENT, taken aback, pulls away)

VINCENT: You're three days late.

PAUL: My trunk here?

VINCENT: Yes, I wrote you. What have you been doing? The train gets in at three in the morning.

PAUL: I went to the café.

VINCENT: I've been at the station three nights in a row. I thought you weren't coming. Last night I went to work on this. (indicates canvas)

PAUL: I had to wait for your brother to send the money. He sold two of my canvases. Thank God for Theo.

VINCENT: You said in your letter you'd be here on the twentieth, three days ago. I've been waiting for you for eight months.

PAUL: (pulls out envelope) "Be not afraid. I bring you tidings of great joy." Our first allowance... from brother Theo!

VINCENT: Paul, you're really here! You look better than I expected-- Theo said you were sick-- You must be tired. Here, sit down. This is your chair.

PAUL: "My" chair?

            (PAUL sits, as VINCENT relieves him of his coat and hat)

VINCENT: I've been out every day. Painting!
Two, sometimes three canvases a day.
Then working in here at night. It's
almost as if I can't stop myself.
(indicating canvases) Look at these
colours. It really looks like that.
Look at this--!

PAUL: (pulls a bottle out of his bag) Yes,
it's beautiful here. Would you like
some of my absinthe?

VINCENT: Yes. Thank you. Now we have
everything. You can live on coffee
and bread, but after-- When you work
out here all day in the sun -- your
mind gets to racing. At night, you
need a few glasses to stun you. The
sun here affects everything. Look out
there. The sun is burning everything
out. Have you ever seen a sun like
that?

PAUL: (mixing absinthe) Yes, in Martinique.
And Panama. Peru.

VINCENT: This sun bleeds into everything, pounds
it down, sucks new colours out of it.
Those gnarled trees in the orchard.
The fields like fire. The people,
too -- darker. Their eyes smoulder.
The wind carves lines in their faces.
You have to fight the elements all the
time, so naturally it leaves you a
little...

            (VINCENT makes gesture for
            "crazy." PAUL hands him a
            glass)

PAUL: To the new work!

VINCENT: The new work. And Theo!

PAUL: And Theo.

     (They toss it back. Pause.
     VINCENT moves to unpack PAUL's
     portfolio)

VINCENT: Now, let's look at these...!

     (VINCENT looks to PAUL, who shrugs
     him on. PAUL wanders about the
     room, takes in VINCENT's copious
     new work -- off-handed yet
     guarded. VINCENT, oblivious,
     lays out PAUL's work on the
     floor. Finally, VINCENT
     discovers "The Vision")

     This is amazing! The space. Full of
     the Spirit.

PAUL: It's Jacob wrestling with the angel.
     I called it "The Vision After The
     Sermon" and offered it to the parish
     church. The priest refused it, of
     course. That painting belongs in a
     sports arena. I'll send it on to Theo
     for the pagan art lovers. (pause)
     It has my special touch. There -- on
     the left.

VINCENT: (spies the praying PAUL figure) That's
     <u>you</u>!

PAUL: Amongst the faithful.

VINCENT: But these outlines...? And such pure colour!

PAUL: (shrugs it off) I see differently in "the clear Breton air."

VINCENT: (stands back to take it all in) These are magnificent. You've changed so much since Paris...I had no idea...

PAUL: You've been working hard, too.

VINCENT: Yes I have. I never worked this way before. Sometimes I squeeze on the oils directly from the tube. Now you can see what I meant in my letters -- what it is I'm driving at!

PAUL: Yes. Very good, Vincent. (pause) I think we can learn a lot from each other. (sits and mixes another absinthe)

VINCENT: It's the beginning. The School of the South... (pause) You should have come right to the house. Sitting up all night in a café...!

PAUL: Last night, while I was waiting, your crony the manager -- Madame Ginoux -- entertained me. "I know you! You are the friend. I recognize you from your portrait." She told me about the lunatic asylum here and the village saint. Some saint! A patron of fools and madmen -- and, I suppose, painters! "Vincent...Vincent the Fool."

VINCENT: "<u>Saint</u> Vincent of the Fools."

PAUL: "King of the Crazies!" We came to the
            right place.

VINCENT: (laughing) The sun makes everyone
            here a little mad. And not just the
            sun, Paul, the wind. The Mistral
            comes about this time of year. Smashes
            you down onto the road, against the
            walls, never lets up. The whole town
            becomes depressed. Or savage. This
            part of the South is ancient, Paul.
            They still practise pagan rituals.
            The Fires of Joy-- You missed it this
            summer!

PAUL: The Fires of Joy?

VINCENT: Women in their costumes, men in rough
            painted wooden masks, blowing on pipes
            and horns, banging on doors and
            shutters. The whole town gathers in
            the square and they build a huge pyre,
            to burn away the pestilence of winter.
            They've done it since the plague in
            the Middle Ages.

PAUL: Christ, no wonder they need a saint to
            watch over them.

VINCENT: People here are simple, but strong in
            their own way. They look out for each
            other. Or they leave each other
            entirely alone.

                    (VINCENT pulls down his canvas of
                     "Roulin" and props it on his own
                     chair)

            This is my good friend, Roulin the
            postmaster.

PAUL: How do you do.

VINCENT: Papa Roulin has been very good to me.
          He helped me find the house, get a fair
          rent. Doesn't he have a gentle face?

PAUL: What are the women like?

VINCENT: I wanted them to pose in their
          costumes, but they're afraid of me.

PAUL: No no. I mean-- (makes a rude and
          obvious gesture)

VINCENT: Oh. Three brothels, because of the
          army garrison. But the women of Arles
          -- the town women -- are very
          reserved. And superstitious.

PAUL: In Brittany, where I was, when a
          barren woman wants a child, she goes
          out into a field where there are
          stones of a very particular shape.
          She goes at night at a certain time of
          the moon. She rubs her naked body on
          the stones. She stays the whole night.
          And sometimes...! (gestures for
          getting pregnant) Of course,
          sometimes...she's not alone.

               (They laugh)

          God forbid merchants should hear of the
          Breton stones -- they would merchandise
          fertility tours!

                    (More laughter. They drink. Long
                    pause. They look directly at
                    each other. A breath of release.
                    They smile, comfortable with one
                    another for the first time)

Vincent.

(Pause. They look around)

VINCENT: A beginning.

PAUL: It's good, Vincent. You're close to something...

VINCENT: You think so? Sometimes--

PAUL: We need to work, together. I need to work with someone who...hnnn. A real painter--! Sometimes I can get -- that! (indicates "The Vision") --and then I don't know what to do with it, how to--

VINCENT: When we've mastered this new place, found a style to paint it--! When our work gets to Paris--! In five years -- together -- we'll make a good living out of this studio. You'll have Mette and your family here with you -- all our friends from Paris -- a colony! A new school. An order of brother artists of the South.

PAUL: Deo Gratias, Brother Vincent, Deo Gratias! But first, let's go to the whorehouse. My blood feels thick, I need a good fucking... Wait. I need something to eat.

VINCENT: There's bread and cold coffee.

PAUL: That's all? Not even a potato?

VINCENT: When I have to eat, I go to the café next door.

PAUL: We should cook for ourselves here in the house. That way, we'll save money. And besides, we'll have better food. Even my enemies acknowledge my mastery in the kitchen.

VINCENT: First!-- I want to show you your room.

PAUL: (groping in bag) Wait, I brought something for you -- here. (hands VINCENT a carving) It's not finished yet.

VINCENT: Oh.

> (VINCENT examines the carving. Pause)

PAUL: Well, where will I sleep?

VINCENT: That's what I was saying, Paul, your room. I've put all the money of the past four weeks into fixing it up so you'd have a proper place to live. My room is yellow. Plain and sturdy. Yours has a large bed, dark wood, with hand-carved endboards. An ivory basin and pitcher on a low red table. And a painted floor -- mauve against the red and white of the walls. (picks up a "Sunflowers" canvas, barely finished, and holds it out to PAUL) And on the walls -- I have only three done up there...I meant to have six...there will be a series of twelve.

PAUL: (gently takes canvas) That's kind of you, Vincent. Very kind. It's a nice room...

VINCENT: (pause) --It's upstairs. (begins to move off)

PAUL: All right, Captain... Wait! Van Gogh, first we should make a few arrangements. about our living situation. Let's take what money you have and what I brought with me...

> (They take out their money. PAUL
> finds a tobacco tin)

...and keep it all in this box. We
plan ahead, spend only what we have,
until Theo's next letter. That way,
we don't run short. Now, what do we
need? Food. You buy the food. I'll
give you a list. I'll do the cooking.
I brought utensils with me. I'll set
the kitchen up. (notices dregs in the
coffee pot; grimaces) Now, coffee.
Where are the beans?

VINCENT: No beans.

> (VINCENT is seated, overwhelmed
> by PAUL's activity)

PAUL: Where's the pot to boil water?

VINCENT: Paul, we can do this later.

PAUL: No. This won't take long.

VINCENT: Don't you think this is a waste of
time?

> (PAUL is already gathering up his
> portfolio works from the floor)

PAUL: I have to take my time. I need to feel
comfortable first, feel my way into it.
Then I can work.

VINCENT: (enthusiastic) You're right!

> (VINCENT joins in the business of
> straightening away the room)

> This should be the main studio. We
> can work with the others in here when
> we have to work indoors... We can
> stack extra canvases in the upstairs
> hallway -- or back of Ginoux's café!

PAUL: (holding out broom to VINCENT) Here.
I always teach my students to master
the large brush strokes first.

VINCENT: (laughs) ...This place won't be big
enough for all of us to live in. The
others will have to lodge in town.

PAUL: Let them sleep under the railway
bridge. It's cheaper, and much more
friendly.

VINCENT: Yes! We're only half a block from the
railway hotel! That way, we can move
crates of artwork directly onto the
train.

PAUL: Keep in mind that anyone arriving here
by that Galloping Goose won't be able
to stand upright -- much less paint --
for at least ten days.

VINCENT: I came here by train, and got right to
work.

PAUL: So your paintings tell me, van Gogh,
so your paintings tell me!

VINCENT laughs.

Act One, Scene Two

BREAKING AWAY

Later. At night. Wine,
cheese, bread. And absinthe.

PAUL: Vincent, I like this house. I've
never lived in a yellow house before.
I was out in the back having a piss
-- and I saw you painted the back wall
yellow! I went around to the front.
You painted the front wall yellow. And
the side is yellow. You crazy Dutchman,
you did it! You got us here together.
This is a dogshit town, but Christ and
other gods be praised, we're not hungry
in Paris tonight.

VINCENT: You're my only friend. I couldn't
start the School without you. You
understand. You know who I am, what
I want. Even Theo -- when I lived
with him -- we couldn't talk. Or
when we did, we'd fight. We'd all
fight. I know now you were my only
friend in Paris. Everyone blamed me
when our boulevard shows failed. I
did all the work. I gave up my
painting, everything, so we could all
benefit. Theo thinks I have no real
talent, I know -- did he tell you that?
I do have talent. Why do people hate
me?

PAUL: People don't hate you. Let me tell you a story... About two years ago -- in December, colder than a merchant's heart -- on the Rue Lepic, a certain man in a sheepskin coat and a rabbitskin hat, and with a red beard -- carrying a painting, still wet, under his arm.

(VINCENT groans)

Ahh! he recognizes himself! What was it? The cap? The beard? Never mind.

VINCENT: I don't remember. Were we together? What did you say to me?

PAUL: No, you didn't see me. I didn't let you. You disappeared into a cheap second-hand shop. I was curious... Much later, I go into the shop, make discreet inquiries about the artist, the painting, the price-- How much did he give you? I forget.

VINCENT: I don't. Five francs.

PAUL: Five? Just five? Anyway, you go into the store -- minutes go by -- and out you come, minus the painting. Ever-curious Gauguin, silent savage, stalks you down the street -- and sees you stopped, just outside the door of your lodging, by a woman--

VINCENT: She was cold...hungry...

PAUL: --and you give her the money from the sale of your painting. What a madman, I thought, what a saint. What a madman, to give it away, within minutes...

VINCENT: Actually, I gave her only half.

PAUL: Well, by God, when I tell it, you'll
            give her the whole five francs! It's
            not a good story if you give her half.
            Otherwise you're only human. In _my_
            story you give her the whole thing.

VINCENT: Just like your painting -- heighten
            for effect.

PAUL: "Style is everything."

VINCENT: (laughs) You spied on me, you sneak!
            But I don't want you to tell anyone.
            It was important to that woman, not
            to me...

                    (PAUL has started to pour wine,
                    but is taken with one of his
                    chills, which lasts only a few
                    seconds. The wine spills across
                    the table)

VINCENT: Paul?

PAUL?   It's -- the fever -- over in a
            minute...

VINCENT: (pause) We must get our health back.
            With the allowance from Theo, we can
            manage a good diet. I get cramps.
            And the pains in my gums are
            sometimes blinding. The doctor gave
            Theo the same instruction as me -- I'm
            supposed to follow it carefully.
            Fresh vegetables. Sleep at regular
            intervals. Always wear a hat in the
            sun. No women. No absinthe. Wine in
            moderation. Refrain from coffee,
            tobacco--!

PAUL: My God, how will we get any work done?

VINCENT: But some day. Some day we will all be
             given new bodies. Strong and enduring.
             Bodies for painting! And women...

PAUL: I like them fat and vicious, Dutchman.
             That's my prescription for endurance.

VINCENT: (concerned) No. I try not to go to
             the houses too often. Not just to
             save the money. More to preserve my
             powers while I have them.

PAUL: You have to feed the fire.

VINCENT: A woman depletes me. Leaves me cold
             for painting. We must practise
             moderation.

                    (PAUL lights his pipe. They sit
                     in quiet memory together, but
                     not together)

             We had a Christ over the dining-room
             table. Looked cold, stern,
             disapproving. The mouth was too thin.
             The painting was there, just above my
             sister. I couldn't wait to leave the
             table.

PAUL: When I was a boy, in Peru, we ate
             midday. Sweets on the sideboard.
             Vases shaped like gods. Such a thing
             for a little boy. Everywhere, things
             from a thousand years ago. Clay pots.
             Gods. Ringing skulls... I never knew
             my father. He died at sea.

VINCENT: Father always shook my hand. He only bothered to do that when I was dressed up, quiet. It is better to have your father die without knowing him, than to have him die, and not be able to say anything.

PAUL: What can you say to a dying person? Just messages to the dead.

VINCENT: I had a brother. Born one year to the day before I was. A brother -- born dead. On his birthday -- our birthday -- we would gather in the churchyard. Father says a prayer. Mother makes us kneel. The stone ...the name. He had my name. Vincent van Gogh.

PAUL: I had a big house in Paris. I used to come home from the brokerage-house about four-thirty or five. Aline, my little daughter, used to jump into my arms. She was the only one to greet me when I came home. Or to say goodbye...

VINCENT: We have to get our health back. We must have strong bodies, practise moderation. That's what the doctor insisted on, for both Theo and me... (trails off)

PAUL: Why?

(Long pause)

VINCENT: It's...a family illness.

PAUL: The pox? (pause) You have syphilis.
            Jesus Christ...

VINCENT: (suddenly agitated, changes the
            subject) I know why we failed in
            Paris. Why we couldn't sell our
            paintings. The whole market is
            controlled. Neo-classicism -- Greek
            temples -- that's what sells. Fourth-
            rate copies of third-rate imitations.
            Dilettantes crammed around a model in
            bathing trunks -- who may have <u>died</u>
            three days before -- no one would
            know! -- glazing and scumbling
            ...chiaroscuro...

PAUL: <u>I</u> was accepted in the Salon. Years
            ago. When I painted correctly "from
            the landscape." I was there, I used
            to paint that way. And I sold. Now
            I paint <u>paintings</u>. And I'm here with
            you. Where do we go now?

VINCENT: We have to teach each other, quickly,
            as we work. Develop a new style.

PAUL: We'll have to sell this new work.

VINCENT: It won't sell. Not <u>yet</u>. It's new.
            People need time. So. We build up
            a stock of paintings with Theo. When
            there's enough done, we show in Paris--

PAUL: And here we are, planning our next show
            instead of painting. Go step by step.

VINCENT: No, you have to give yourself over to
            the whole vision. You can't play by
            the rules when you're trying to make
            new ones... When I was finally

allowed to preach the Gospel -- my
chosen work -- in the Borinage -- the
coal mines -- in a corner of the earth
where men were broken, barely alive.
Labouring under the earth in darkness...
Prepared sermons? Words can't mend
twisted bones and diseased lungs. I
had to show them that God's love was
real. It was there all the time. In
me. I was cloaked in fine starched
cotton and fine words-- "If you have
two coats and your neighbour has
none"--?! I closed my Bible,
distributed my possessions, moved
into a miner's shack. I ate with
them. I worked with them. I taught
their children. And when the shaft
collapsed -- one hundred and twenty-
six men, and boys, were buried in
that mine -- and over a hundred more
were maimed and injured--

> (PAUL has been digging away at a
> carving while listening. He
> gets up to fetch another chisel,
> and notices the camera. VINCENT
> turns away, growing intense and
> isolated in his story)

But we were not alone. There was
Christian comfort and love. The
Church. Two senior ministers of the
Church came at the time of the
disaster. Came to inspect me. To see
if I was proceeding step by proper
step in my mission. How could I
live like that, they asked, as if I
were just another wretched miner?
Should I not be an example the people
could look up to? They blaspheme

against their own Christ. Did He not
turn out the money-lenders who
defiled the temple? As I turned <u>them</u>
away in His name. Threw the fine
linen collar in their teeth. <u>I</u>
dismissed <u>them</u> in their hypocrisy.
Ungodliness!

> (PAUL has made himself ready to
> take a photograph of VINCENT.
> He stands under a cloth cowl
> behind his tripod, the flash
> powder in a pan held in his
> outstretched arm. He calls
> ominously)

PAUL: <u>Vincent van Gogh</u>!

> (VINCENT turns, startled. He
> realizes what is happening,
> and abruptly turns his back to
> the camera as PAUL detonates
> the flash powder. PAUL is
> pleased)

PAUL: Excellent. "Van Gogh Turns His Back
On Paris and Looks South."

VINCENT: (turning to face PAUL) What are you
doing?

PAUL: Making "fine portraits" for the
parlour.

VINCENT: You can't take my picture--!

PAUL: Let the camera have its day, too.
<u>You</u> can paint yourself any way you
like.

VINCENT: But people will compare. (gestures at
            paintings) If I line up twenty self-
            portraits, each one will be valid in
            its own way. There's no record of
            the model. With a photograph, they'll
            see what I've done.

PAUL: Yes. They're lies, Vincent, these
            portraits of yourself. Beautiful
            lies. So, the camera lies too. Let
            it.

VINCENT: No, no, the paintings are unique.

PAUL: Yes, they are. But we don't need to
            make records any more. The camera
            will do that for us. Family portraits,
            landscapes. Now we can paint new art.
            What's in your head. Your heart.
            Where they can't go. Oh, they'll try.
            By God, they'll try to invent a
            camera to go in there. But they can't.
            They never will. We're the only ones
            who can.

VINCENT: Then this doesn't belong here.

PAUL: It is here. Now. New materials.
            New forms. Machinery.

VINCENT: Yes, cities choked with dirt, noise,
            confusion. Nowhere to live!
            Everything too big, too fast...

PAUL: That's what Paris celebrates, Vincent.
            Progress. Look. The Exposition next
            year? They want to show the rest of
            Europe they're first. And best. So.
            They're erecting a tower of bare metal
            beams to stand over them like a
            colossus. Guarding the entire city.

VINCENT: A fortress.

PAUL: No. It's empty! Nowhere to live on
             it. In it. Totally useless.

                  (PAUL and VINCENT lean on one
                     another. They are both, by now,
                     quite drunk)

             But it has one purpose: an aviary.
             Get the pigeons off the street!
             Thousands of white vultures. A rain
             of pigeon guano hurled down across
             Montmartre!

VINCENT: The vengeance of God.

PAUL: A savage God. Confusion. Anarchy!

VINCENT: A confusion of tongues... It's a
             Tower of Babel!

PAUL: Yes! The great tower!

                  (PAUL sets out to build the
                     Eiffel Tower. He forages about
                     for materials, clears the table
                     and uses it for the foundation.
                     PAUL and VINCENT urge each other
                     on as VINCENT "preaches" from
                     the Book of Genesis)

PAUL: VINCENT:

                              The whole earth of one
                              language, and one
                              speech...
                              And they said to one
                              another, "Go to.

Go to!

PAUL:	VINCENT:
	Let us build us a city and a tower,
A tower! Let us build us a tower!	
	whose top may reach unto heaven."
A tower! Let us build us a tower! Build us a tower!	
	And the Lord saw this, and He said:
Build us a tower!	
	"Behold, this they begin to do, and now nothing will be restrained from them which they have imagined to do.
Nothing will be restrained! What they have imagined to do!	
	Go to," the Lord said,
Go to!	
	"Go to, let Us go down, and there confound their language,
Give us Gods! Confound us!	
	that they may not understand
Give us more Gods!	

PAUL: VINCENT:

                               one another's speech."

Gods of metal!
Colossus God Pigeons!

                               God Pigeons!

Gods of shit!

                               God shit!

A rain of God ca-ca
God ca-ca!   God ca-ca.
Caw-caw.
Caw! Caw!   Caw-caw!
Caw! Caw-caw! Caaww!
Caaaaaaaawwwwwhhhhh!!   Caw--!

                   (Abruptly, at this point of climax
                   -- the camera on its tripod now
                   the top of the completed "Eiffel
                   Tower" -- the camera topples from
                   its housing and crashes to the
                   ground. The spell is broken, as
                   the rest of the tower crumbles)

PAUL: (laughing, catching his breath) Damn!
                   ...damn...

                   (Both are exhausted. VINCENT,
                   stunned and confused by the debris,
                   slumps over and slides into a
                   heavy sleep. PAUL is left
                   standing amid the chaos. He loses
                   interest in the broken camera)

PAUL: If a crow could feed in quiet, it would
                   have more meat. Well, I can't be quiet.
                   Neither can he. So. Here we are...
                   Caw.
                   I would like to be a pig. Only man is
                   capable of being ridiculous. Yes, a

wise pig, with beautiful eyes and long
lashes. Mister Pig. Once I told a
prudish Dane of the Japanese custom of
families bathing together. I thought
him intelligent. "But your Japanese
are vulgar pigs!" Yes. But in the
pig all is good.

I am a wolf, lean and collarless. The
animal in me...

Once upon a time, the wild animals,
the really big ones, used to leap and
roar. Today they are stuffed...

The animal in me...

Civilized people! You are proud of not
eating human flesh. If you were cast
adrift on the ocean on a raft, and
starving, you would eat it. On the
other hand, every day you eat your
neighbour's heart.

Two men in me, one savage, one
civilized. Little by little I have
closed my heart to sensitive feelings,
in order to preserve my moral strength.
Two temperaments in me: the savage
and the sensitive. The sensitive has
disappeared. I am strong.

(PAUL is now dreaming awake)

In my dream, I make a fortune with my
circus, the greatest circus in the
world. Every night I enter the big
cat cage, watched by a huge crowd.
First I work the lion, the lioness.
I make them roar and leap, with my whip

and prod. I wallow in their odours.
The animal in me is satiated.

Now, in my dream, the cage is empty.
Then the great royal tiger is with
me. He demands my caress. He shows
me, by signs with his whiskers and
fangs, when he has had enough. He
loves me. He is scornful. I dare
not beat him. I am afraid of him,
and he knows it. He takes advantage
of my fear. The fear makes me happy.
I quiver with it.

At night my wife seeks my caresses.
She knows I am afraid of her and she
takes advantage of my fear. Is there
happiness without pain?

At night, by lamplight, in my dream,
I watch the stupid, cowardly crowd,
which craves death and carnage. They
are curious for the spectacle of
chains and the whip, slavery and the
prod. They gorge on the howls and
screams. They are never satiated.
The circus band breaks into harsh
and discordant sounds. Two men in
the crowd, Lords of Creation, kick,
and strike each other with their
fists.
The trained monkeys will not imitate
them.

Lights fade to black.

Act One, Scene Three

WORKING TOGETHER

This is a sequence of six
scenes representing a few
weeks of daily work outdoors.
Transitions between individual
scenes are effected through
the lighting.

1. First day. Bright sun.
On the hillside overlooking
the fields. VINCENT is
discovered at his easel, with
a finished canvas. Paul
enters, with gear.

PAUL: Halloo!

             (PAUL begins to set up. VINCENT
             comes over, with canvas)

VINCENT: There, look at that! That's what I was
             trying to get: the sun pushing the
             ground down around the trees, so the
             trees are pushed up.

PAUL: They're stuck together with all that
             ochre.

VINCENT: Yes, like hands...veins... That's why
             I left out the harvesters: the trees
             are the figures.

PAUL: Like crippled beggars.

(VINCENT is pleased)

You changed the light.

VINCENT: The sun wasn't doing what I needed, to
           bring out the fields. This way the
           light lifts the trees.

PAUL: It works. But I thought your credo
           was to paint realistically from the
           scene.

VINCENT: And <u>heighten</u> what's there. But it has
           to <u>be</u> there, or I couldn't see it.

PAUL: (considers this) Well, back to work...

           (VINCENT moves back to his easel
           and calls over his shoulder)

VINCENT: It's finished! I'm going to work up
           another canvas, <u>closer</u> to the wagons.
           Get the women binding and the men with
           their forks...the labour of
           harvesting... That broken-down
           haycart--!

PAUL: (calling back) See you in three hours.

           (to the audience) Vincent has to learn
           to finish a canvas. He works too fast,
           doesn't let what he sees work on him.
           But he <u>does</u> draw on his imagination,
           improvises. If only he would trust it.

           (PAUL puts the blank canvas on his
           easel, and begins to consider the
           available view. VINCENT "writes"
           to his brother-dealer)

VINCENT: Dear Theo-- We should have some dozen canvases for you in about two weeks' time. The hot weather has Paul in good spirits, and he's throwing himself into the new work!

> (VINCENT forages in his paintbox, and assesses his finished canvas. Both men mutter to themselves as they "work")

PAUL: VINCENT:

horizon too high
less of the hill
wider   Japanese
flatten it out

                                    change the browns

complementary colours?

                                    to yellow

just on the right

> 2. Two days later. Fair day but not as bright. Another location.
>
> PAUL stands back from his canvas, stares at it intently. VINCENT stands away from PAUL at his sketch-box, watching. He cautiously approaches PAUL and stands beside him. A pause. PAUL examines the sketches in his hand, the painting again, then tosses

the sketches away in defeat.
PAUL, at his paintbox, takes
a cloth, wipes his hands.
VINCENT picks up PAUL's
sketches, examines them along
with the canvas.

PAUL: (offhand, yet final) Enough of this.
Let's go back.

(VINCENT is absorbed in PAUL's
canvas)

VINCENT: No, it can work.

PAUL: Forget it. (pause) Don't you think?
I tried to put the three together.
Doesn't fit.

VINCENT: (grasping the concept) No. Not right
away. May I?

(PAUL hands him the charcoal.
VINCENT draws on PAUL's canvas,
glancing repeatedly at the view.
Pause)

It all grows out of the earth. Wheat.
(pause; still drawing) That clump of
rocks...figures. But not there. There.
Figures grow out of the ground too...
the legs. They have weight because
they draw it up from the earth.
(continues to draw) It's all of a
piece, like weaving. (finished) Now.
Now you change the lines. Separate
the shapes, strengthen them.

PAUL: (pointing) · Here?

VINCENT: (making bold lines with his finger) Yes.
From the whole pattern...draw it out.
You can't paste it together with pieces
from a sketchbook!

(VINCENT hands PAUL the charcoal,
turns to go)

PAUL: (firm but excited) Thank you, Vincent.
Thank you.

(VINCENT turns, smiles at PAUL,
returns to his own work. PAUL
tackles the canvas with a new
vigour)

PAUL: (to audience) How does he do it? Lives
and works in all that frenzy, and --
line -- line -- line! Two days of bad
work solved in two minutes! I must be
getting old!

(PAUL laughs. Tossing off his
sun-hat, he paints away)

VINCENT: Dear Theo-- We are making great strides.
Paul and I have much to learn from one
another. We are certain that a new
technique <u>can</u> be developed here in the
South. (returns to work)

PAUL: (muttering)   VINCENT: (muttering)

not enough orange
more yellow

green tints

even more
right
no

still no bite
lighten the blue?

                        some ochre

there!

                      3. Some days later. Bright
                      sun returns. At the bridge
                      over the river, with
                      washerwomen.

VINCENT: Let's move. We're too close.

PAUL: I'm fine. I want the women flat on.

VINCENT: If we paint them from this angle,
               they'll appear too large against the
               bridge. (notices PAUL's canvas) Try
               alizarin down the sides of the trees.
               Lift them off the blue.

PAUL: The trees don't have to fly.
               (concentrates)

VINCENT: But they're stuck flat against the
               hillside that way.

PAUL: Bravo.

VINCENT: You can't do that...I wouldn't do that.

PAUL: No. You wouldn't.

VINCENT: And the river. Where's the blue
               cerulean? And crimson -- against
               those viridians?

PAUL: They're still in their tubes. I'm
          painting washerwomen, not a travel
          advertisement.

VINCENT: Your river looks like a sewer!

PAUL: It _is_ a sewer. They're doing their
          laundry in it.

VINCENT: (resigned) Well, I'm moving. If I
          paint from here, the women will be too
          large and I'll lose the bridge.

PAUL: (irritated) You can paint it from
          here. Then we can share the paintboxes.

          (VINCENT turns to go. PAUL puts
          down his brushes)

I want you to stand over there. Stand
over there. Look at the bridge...
Now, stand here... Now, I want you to
paint _that_.

          (No response)

What you saw.

          (No response)

Close your eyes... Close your eyes!...
Now. See the bridge, and the women,
down on the left, small, like you want
them. Open your eyes... Now, dream --
with your eyes open!

          (PAUL is crouched in front of
          VINCENT, gazing intently at the
          view)

VINCENT: (growing angry) Paul, I can't work.
You're standing in my way.

PAUL: Aye, aye, Captain. (returns to his
canvas)

VINCENT: (defiantly) I know my work and I know
my limits! We'll see when both canvases
are done. We'll compare them -- which
one conveys the view.

PAUL: (in dismissal) <u>Aye, aye, Captain</u>!
(to audience) It's the only way to shut
Vincent up. Agree with him. Sometimes
he's right. It doesn't matter. But if
he'd listen to <u>me</u>, he wouldn't keep
painting the same painting. (returns to
his painting)

VINCENT: Dear Theo-- Paul has ideas about
landscape which are quite extraordinary.
He takes great risks. But he often runs
aground on his own theories. He has yet
to paint <u>directly</u> with a sure hand.
(returns to work)

PAUL: (muttering)   VINCENT: (muttering)

too many shrubs
take one out?
no
what's missing?

                          touch of lemon

(growls)
red! no red
red what?
bush

                          vermilion!

far right
against the grey tree

> 4. Several days later. Dark
> and overcast. Heavy wind.
>
> PAUL struggles to keep his
> canvas in place.

PAUL: (snarls and groans) Couldn't we work
             at home? This wind is impossible!!

> (VINCENT comes over to PAUL's
> paintbox)

VINCENT: Let me have some sienna.

PAUL: What happened to yours?

VINCENT: It's on the canvas. We should grind
             more colour from now on.

PAUL: You should carry twice as much with you.

VINCENT: (forages; then suddenly) What's wrong
             with the way I paint? I have to put
             the paint on thickly to show the energy.
             I have to show the weight of the earth.
             Move paint the way the wind moves the
             trees.

> (VINCENT shouts to be heard
> against the wind)

Look at what the wind's doing!! The
purples and reds -- the underside of
the leaves!

PAUL: The wind is blowing us off our feet!!

VINCENT: That's why you should stake your easel
            to the ground! The mistral <u>helps</u> you
            paint! It's like the sailor tied to
            the mast -- you sail right into the
            painting!!

PAUL: Damn! There's <u>sand</u> in my paint!!

               (The canvas blows out of PAUL's
                hands and is destroyed)

            <u>I'm going home</u>!!

                       PAUL grabs his gear and
                       leaves. Oblivious, VINCENT
                       remains, painting.

                       5. Late afternoon. Warm light,
                       no wind.

                       Quiet work. PAUL painting at
                       his easel, VINCENT pulling wine
                       bottle from the sack. VINCENT
                       pours PAUL a cup, takes it over
                       to him, waits for him to stop
                       work. PAUL notices VINCENT,
                       stops, sees the mug.

PAUL: (happy for the break) Tea-time?

                   (VINCENT settles, drinks from the
                    bottle. PAUL lights pipes for
                    both of them)

VINCENT: Ahh, all those ladies in their long
white dresses. Looking at landscapes.
Drinking out of silver tea services.
In London...the Print Room at Goupil's
-- when I sold pictures--

PAUL: Did you sell a lot?

VINCENT: Oh yes. Until I started to talk about
art... A woman came in -- very fat.
Ears at the back of her head! There was
an armchair in the middle of the salon,
where you could sit, and take in an
entire wall of prints. Nothing special
on the wall, of course. She sat -- the
chair disappeared. And she examined the
display. Wondering just which pictures
would go best with her fat furniture,
her fat draperies, and her fat dog. She
picked one of a dog. When I criticized
it, she was incensed! She gasped all
over the manager, and stormed out. I
would like to show her one of your
paintings! Now that's something you
could paint, Paul, a dog. Put a dog in
there. A fat dog!

PAUL: "Jacob Wrestling with the Fat Dog"?

VINCENT: "Battle of the Ten Naked Fat Dogs."

PAUL: (striking a pose) "Mrs. Siddons as a
Tragic Fat Dog."

VINCENT: (grotesque pose) "The Martyrdom of
Saint Sebastian... (smaller) and Fat
Dog."

PAUL: "Fat Dog Contemplating a Bust of Homer."

VINCENT: --"Aristotle Contemplating a Bust--

TOGETHER: --of Fat Dog"!

VINCENT: "Mona Fat Dog"?-- (supplicant to PAUL)
            "Presentation of the Fat Dog in the
            Temple"!!

PAUL: (taking the "gift" and humping it)
            --"Leda and the Fat Dog"!!

            (They collapse in laughter)

VINCENT: (laughing) No no, all people want are
            pretty pictures. When they come in--?
            They know what they want to buy.

PAUL: They do, yes.

VINCENT: Not the people who like our work...

PAUL: Who's that? Just other painters.

VINCENT: Painters don't like paintings. They
            like to argue about painting. I could
            show our work to any five of us back in
            Paris and get five entirely different
            verdicts. Seurat! (imitating Seurat)
            But van Gogue, such chaos. You must
            begin again. Lay out each colour, mix
            to mathematical ratio. Precision,
            van Gogue, prismatics.

PAUL: Lautrec! (on his knees, as Lautrec,
            PAUL approaches the easel, peers
            between the legs) But you've painted
            nothing this week, Vincent?! (discovers
            the canvas above his head) Ah!... But
            -- where are the women, the ladies of
            the night?? You must begin again. Too

> much yellow, Vincent, too much yellow.
> Flesh, we must have flesh!! (slavers)

VINCENT: (as Manet) ...Interesting...
Promise...

> (PAUL shouts "Manet!")

...I made somewhat the same mistakes...
Begin again.

PAUL: Give me your hat... (puts on hat;
imitates VINCENT) How can you say that?
Why did you say that? When did you say
that? How did you say that? Did you
say that?

VINCENT: (a mixed response) That's me!

PAUL: (himself again) Of course, Monsignor
Manet never deigned to appear at our
exhibitions. But then, can you imagine
Manet coming to a working-class
restaurant to see art?

> (Returning to playing VINCENT,
> PAUL takes VINCENT -- as Manet --
> by the arm)

You must see this, this is the new art,
no matter where it hangs -- oops!
careful of the spilt wine! No, no,
no, no, the painting hangs <u>over</u> the
table, not <u>on</u> the table -- move that
over here by the cash -- come on, you
have to work together -- now, Mr. Manet,
you can sit here and view the new art.
Mr. Manet -- Mr. Manet? <u>Why don't you
understand?!</u> (as himself) He was
right, you know. It <u>was</u> mad. You were

a fool to think you could pull off a
modern exhibition in a run-down eatery.

VINCENT: What do you mean "a fool"?

PAUL: Not you. The idea -- the idea was
            foolish. No -- you and Theo organized
            it -- and you both did a fine job.
            But it couldn't work.

VINCENT: You never told me that. And you
            certainly went out of your way to seize
            the lion's share of wall space for
            yourself. More than anyone.

PAUL: Seurat paints too slowly. And too big.
            Lautrec didn't need the money.

VINCENT: Cezanne did. You didn't push for him.

PAUL: No, because Theo did. Besides, Cezanne
            had outsold me by a generous margin.
            It was my turn to sell something.

VINCENT: Selling doesn't make a painting valid.

PAUL: Not selling doesn't either. Vincent,
            it really was mad. Paintings, modern
            no less, in a slum restaurant! Better
            not to show at all.

VINCENT: <u>You</u> seemed anxious enough to hang.

PAUL: Hang indeed.

VINCENT: It was worth the attempt. Better than
            nothing.

PAUL: You fool, you lost a month's painting
            time organizing that little disaster.
            And no one bought.

VINCENT: A month? I lost a year! Arguing with painters who were too busy being their own worst enemies to have any chance at success. Success through united action.

PAUL: To the barricades!

VINCENT: That's right! This is war.

PAUL: Aye, aye, Captain.

VINCENT: We have to help each other, just to survive. That's why we quit Paris and came here, to start this colony together. To do good work, without the competition and the bickering--!

                (VINCENT recognizes his own pitch,
                stops himself. Pause, then PAUL
                speaks quietly)

PAUL: Sometimes, just being able to paint seems enough. Sometimes.

                They hold firm eye contact,
                then turn away, in recognition
                if not resolution.

                6. Very late afternoon. Cold,
                dim. The cold weather is upon
                us.

                VINCENT is asleep. PAUL is
                gripped by his chills. He is
                stricken by a sudden seizure.
                He mutters over and over again
                "God -- God -- God." Clenched

                    teeth chatter. It peaks,
                    suddenly is over. PAUL gulps
                    wine from the bottle. VINCENT
                    wakens. PAUL flops down.

PAUL: No constipation and regular fucking and
            a man could pull through.

VINCENT: Why did you let me fall asleep after
            lunch?

PAUL: You needed sleep.

VINCENT: I don't need to sleep. I need to paint.

PAUL: It's too windy.

VINCENT: I told you -- stake your easel to the
            ground.

PAUL: Let's go. I don't feel well.

VINCENT: There's only a few days of good weather
            left. After that we'll have to work
            indoors all the time.

PAUL: No. I have the fever today. Besides,
            I need the time to think.

VINCENT: There'll be plenty of time to think,
            and work, inside all you want later on.
            If we miss the good weather, it's gone!
            (resumes painting with fervour)

PAUL: To hell with you, van Gogh. It's taken
            me this long since the fever in
            Martinique to work every day again.
            I'm going to work at my own pace,
            finish my paintings, stay healthy.
            Damned mistral!

PAUL storms off. VINCENT,
painting, ignores him.
Blackout.

Act One, Scene Four.

CANDLE HAT

Late evening in the darkened
house. VINCENT lights a
circle of candles, which are
fastened to the brim of a
straw hat, and places the hat
on his head. He goes to his
easel and begins painting.
PAUL enters, drunk, singing
incoherently, possibly in
Spanish.

PAUL: Vincent! What are you doing?

VINCENT: We're out of kerosene.

PAUL: (sings, celebrating VINCENT's "halo")

            Veni creator spiritus
            Mentes tuorum visita...

O Saint Vincent, Patron of Fools, help
me in my misery. For I have not done
a painting since last Wednesday.

Through my fault, through my fault,
through my most grievous fault. How
many paintings have <u>you</u> done since
Wednesday, Vincent? Six? Eight?

    (No answer. PAUL begins a hymn)

My dearest friends,
Standing with me in this holy light,
Join with me in asking God for mercy.

    (PAUL begins to pound rhythmically
    on the table-top)

Give me a drink. Give me a drink. A
drink. Give me a drink...

    (VINCENT is forced to leave his
    painting. He pours wine into a
    paint mortar, as there are no
    glasses at hand. He hands it to
    PAUL)

PAUL: You dumb dog. There's paint in here!

VINCENT: Just drink it. And get some kerosene.
You're the only one who can. We have
no money left. And I can't charm
Madame Ginoux like you can.

    (PAUL begins to sketch VINCENT,
    who is still wearing his candle
    hat)

<u>I</u> can't go. I'm working on this canvas
and I can't stop. (thrusts bottle in
PAUL's face) Here. Go to the café and
fill this with kerosene.

            (PAUL's drawing fails. He throws
               it to the floor)

You can't do that. You didn't pay for
it. My brother did. We can't afford
to waste.

            (Indignant, PAUL picks up the
            discarded sheet and carefully
            tears it into several pieces)

(incensed) It's _my_ house. _My_ floor.
_My_ paper.

PAUL: Stupid baby. Theo takes care of his
           baby brother.

VINCENT: I'm his _older_ brother!

PAUL: Go away.

VINCENT: Maybe _you_ should go.

PAUL: --All right...!

            (PAUL staggers away. VINCENT,
            his candle hat still alight,
            steps between PAUL and the
            doorway, grasping for persuasive
            arguments)

VINCENT: You can't leave! --If you go away,
            there'll never be a School of the
            South... _You're_ the teacher -- the
            new painters won't come to me... Paul,
            if you leave now, your family will never
            be able to join you. And Theo -- if you
            go, Theo won't support us. He's taking
            a gamble on us when no one else will.
            How can we afford to jeopardize his

career? And how can we paint without
his allowance? This is my last chance,
Paul. I've failed at everything else.
I'm a painter and I have to paint. And
so do you. Here. In Arles.

> (PAUL has been thwarted in several
> attempts to find a clear path to
> the doorway. VINCENT now has
> PAUL trapped in a corner. PAUL
> stares at the dripping candles,
> overwhelmed)

PAUL: ...I'll go and get the kerosene.

> VINCENT, content, turns to
> resume work. PAUL grabs the
> bottle, passes behind VINCENT,
> and abruptly blows out all the
> candles on the hat. Quick fade
> to black as PAUL exits.

Act One, Scene Five

TRAPPED INDOORS

> Inside the house. Several days
> later. VINCENT is upset by the
> wind, the cold, and by being
> cooped up in the house by the
> weather. He sets up sunflowers
> in a vase and begins to paint
> them. PAUL crashes into the

space from outdoors, in cold
weather clothes, blowing and
cheerful. He puts down an
armload of food.

PAUL: Wine. Bread. Coffee. I spent it all.
Make it last till the money comes.

(VINCENT eats, goes back to
work. PAUL removes most of his
outside clothing. He sets
up to paint)

PAUL: (to audience) For two weeks we are
confined to our yellow house by the
mistral, the cold. It is not possible
to work outdoors in this wind.

(VINCENT glowers at PAUL)

Vincent's face is falling off. I
paint it.

(PAUL puts a canvas onto his
easel. VINCENT comes to warm
his hands at the stove. He sees
PAUL's painting of him,
"Vincent Painting Sunflowers."

VINCENT goes to the painting and
looks at it. He seems pleased.
They smile at each other. PAUL
shrugs. VINCENT goes back to
work with a new energy.

VINCENT is thinking. He stops
painting. He gets up and takes
a second look. He is puzzled.
He returns to work.

VINCENT works in a broken rhythm.
He stops and goes once more to the
stove, on the pretext of warming
his hands. Surreptitiously, he
looks at PAUL's painting. He
spies. Finally he speaks)

VINCENT: That's me. But I look crazy.

(PAUL does not respond)

You're painting me.

PAUL: I'm painting a painting.

VINCENT: I don't want to look like that.

PAUL: It's not a photograph.

(VINCENT goes back to his easel,
but cannot work)

VINCENT: You're spying on me!

PAUL: Don't be foolish.

VINCENT: I won't let you paint me that way.

PAUL: I've done it.

(PAUL continues to paint. VINCENT
sits. He can't paint. He is
stymied. Abruptly, he takes his
rag and scrapes his canvas, as he
can't scrape PAUL's. PAUL stops
painting. VINCENT stomps across
the room, grabs his cap and coat,
nearly knocking PAUL's canvas off
the easel as he crosses to the
door, and storms out. PAUL
speaks as VINCENT passes)

Vincent...

> VINCENT is gone. PAUL looks
> at his canvas, shrugs and
> grumbles, returns to work.
> Fade to black.

Act One, Scene Six

MONEY

> The next morning. PAUL is
> sketching one of VINCENT's
> canvases when VINCENT, in coat
> and cap, enters carrying a
> letter. VINCENT sees PAUL
> and stops in his tracks. PAUL
> immediately closes his sketch-
> book, goes to the table and
> sits. An uncomfortable pause.

PAUL: How much this time?

> (VINCENT moves to the table,
> opening the envelope. PAUL takes
> the money to count and verify as
> VINCENT paces, reading over
> Theo's letter)

VINCENT: A hundred francs... Theo says he's
          just about to move... This is all he

                      can afford... He can't promise any
                      more for at least three weeks!

PAUL: Damn.

VINCENT: We're more important than his creditors!
                      How can he do this?

PAUL: The problem is not his creditors.

VINCENT: Then what? (struggles with his coat)

PAUL: The problem is Johanna.

VINCENT: They're engaged, yes. But at this
                      point -- a marriage is out of the
                      question.

PAUL: Really? What makes you think that a
                      good Dutch girl like Johanna wants to
                      support you and me?

VINCENT: No, no. She has nothing to do with
                      this. She's merely a fiancée...

PAUL: Merely?!

VINCENT: How could he afford to support all three
                      of us? -- four?

                            (Distraught, VINCENT slaps his
                            coat onto a peg)

PAUL: We'll have to make do. (arranging the
                      bills in piles) Thirty for rent.
                      Forty for food. Ten for wine and
                      tobacco. And women. Twenty for
                      supplies.

                            (VINCENT, who has joined PAUL,
                            sits across from him)

VINCENT: Twenty's not enough. Take ten off food for canvas.

(PAUL shifts a ten-franc note)

I forgot. We still owe money. The woman who sold me your bed had to be paid three weeks ago.

PAUL: How much?

VINCENT: Twenty francs.

PAUL: (taking another two bills from food pile) Anything else?

VINCENT: I still owe ten for frames.

PAUL: All right. No food. We start with no food.

(PAUL sweeps the table clean and counts out only three piles)

VINCENT: That's not enough. There's never enough. We have to send more paintings.

PAUL: Tell me. Van Gogh. Exactly. What is your arrangement with your brother? What does he send you? How many paintings do you send him?

VINCENT: A portion of all that I do...

PAUL: A portion. How many paintings in a portion?

VINCENT: Half.

PAUL: Half? My God. Theo agreed to support me for one canvas a month. Why can't he do that for you?

VINCENT: You don't understand. Theo is not an
art dealer. He's my <u>brother</u>. Theo
pulled me from the coal mines, healed
me, brought me to Paris. It was Theo
who showed me the new art, Theo who
paid my way in the studios, Theo who
tried to sell my work. I lived under
his roof. I ate his food, I stole his
sleep, I used his woman, I <u>used</u> him.
Theo's health is bad now. He's in
debt because he supported me. I should
be supporting him. And I can't. I'm
a painter now. Both of us, Theo and I,
paint my paintings. Years, and years...
Six years.

PAUL: So? It was his choice.

VINCENT: But I <u>owe</u> him -- we have to pay him
back. <u>We</u> make the paintings now. We
send them to Theo. Good paintings,
paintings he can sell. We support him,
care for him--

PAUL: He's your brother, yes. But he's my
dealer, Vincent. I'm keeping my part
of the bargain.

VINCENT: Are you? What does Theo have of ours
to sell -- right now?? He has no money
left. We're not sending him enough.
We have to send more. Send him those
two canvases you're working on!

PAUL: They're not finished.

VINCENT: Then finish them. Today. <u>Now</u>!

PAUL: This is not a factory.

VINCENT: (slapping at the table) <u>Send them</u>!

PAUL: (firmly) Theo is not our boss. He
            supports us. He believes in us. He
            wants us to do our best work. And
            that takes time.

                    (VINCENT slams down his hand, just
                     missing PAUL, leaps to his feet,
                     and wheels around)

VINCENT: You spend our money! You fuck! You
            get sick! You talk, you only talk.
            And you don't <u>paint</u>!!-- You make <u>me</u>
            do the work.... I've been doing this
            for eight months while you sat in
            Britanny. I do twelve paintings a
            week -- more! And I put this School
            together. And I'm keeping it together.
            And I'll do it alone if I have to.

PAUL: Aye, aye, Captain.

VINCENT: (explodes) <u>Don't laugh at me</u>!

                    (PAUL, rising abruptly from his chair,
                     nearly topples the table)

PAUL: <u>Van Gogh, God damn you</u>. You can't tell
            me how to work. I'm not your brother.
            I'm not your houseboy. And I sure as
            hell am not your goddamned student!

VINCENT: (shocked, but resisting) Then work
            <u>with</u> me!

PAUL: Now you -- you step back -- you are
            pushing too hard -- you can't run <u>me</u>--

VINCENT: You're wasting time. You're wasting <u>my</u>
            time. I'm the one who's sick -- sicker
            than you are. I have syphilis. <u>I</u> have
            the fever, the shakes, the blind pain.

I hear voices -- I can't see! (abrupt
pause; then lower) I'm _dying_. I
don't have years...I have months. I
have _no time_.

PAUL: _You_ have syphilis. _You_ have no time.
That's not _my_ problem. _I_ have time.

VINCENT: _We're failing_!!

PAUL: (sits again) I'm not a failure. I
have no doubts about my work, no doubts
about its place, no doubts about my
future--

VINCENT: Doubts? _I_ have doubts. (turns and
grabs coffee pot) Look. Look at this.
Empty. That's a doubt. (slams pot
onto table, grabs a cooking pot) And
this. Another doubt. (slams it down,
grabs food cannister) And here's
another doubt! (slams it down, grabs
an empty glass) And this--!!

    (PAUL leaps to his feet, facing
    VINCENT squarely)

PAUL: _Shut up_!! Shut. Up.

    VINCENT is stunned. Then he
    places the glass on the table
    with exaggerated care. VINCENT
    crosses to his chair, throwing
    himself into it. PAUL sits.
    They are now facing away from
    each other. Impasse. Fade to
    black.

Act Two, Scene One

THE SULK

> There has been silence for
> three days. VINCENT is
> seated in his chair, his back
> to PAUL. He smokes his pipe,
> does not move or make any
> response. PAUL counters with
> the cheerful ritual of shaving,
> with towel, basin, and
> straight-edge razor. He sits
> at the table, behind VINCENT
> watching him, and needles him
> with his singing of a lyrical
> Breton air.

PAUL: (sings)
               I wish O Son
               I wish O Son of the Living God
               I wish O Son of the Living God
                 For a secret hut to be my
                   dwelling.

               A beautiful wood
               A beautiful wood close by around it
               A beautiful wood close by around it
                 On every side to shelter and hide
                   it.

And a lovely church
And a lovely church decked out with
  linen
And a lovely church decked out with
  linen
    A dwelling for the God of Heaven.

My fill of clothing
My fill of clothing and of food
My fill of clothing and of food
    From the King of Good Fame.

    (PAUL is finished. VINCENT's only
    response has been to take himself,
    and his chair, to a safer corner
    of the room. PAUL is determined.
    He sets us his camera on its
    tripod and makes as if he is
    taking VINCENT's photo. VINCENT,
    spying, hastily turns away in his
    chair. PAUL pursues the joke,
    fetching VINCENT's coat and straw
    hat, and propping them over the
    tripod, until the camera apparatus
    is clearly a pathetic scarecrow
    version of VINCENT. With a brush
    held at the end of one coat sleeve,
    PAUL makes the scarecrow walk
    about and stab at a canvas, as
    if to paint)

Oh Paul, help me. I can't paint.
Yellow, yellow, yellow. Oh Paul, look,
I'm trying to paint today. Oh, help...

    (VINCENT steadfastly refuses to
    acknowledge the goad. PAUL gives
    up. He sits at the table, and
    finishes a letter he has been
    writing to his wife)

Dear Mette-- Greetings from Arles. I
am sorry not to have written you
earlier, but I have been very busy
trying to make this new project work.
Arles is a pretty town, but it is now
mistral season. Very cold. And the
wind blows. And blows. And blows. We
have been inside for two weeks... And
silent for three days. I fear the sun
is dead. Vincent is quite the soldier.
Very reserved. He is having some
difficulty with his work just now, but
with my help I am sure he will recover.
I hope you have received the monies
from the sale of my ceramics, as I have
asked Theo van Gogh to send it on to
you. It is not much. It is hard for
you, yes. For me too. To be without
the children, for one thing. I miss
them so, and weep for them. Children,
at least, love absolutely, and ask
nothing in return. I want to have us
all together again. Surely you can
understand that. Would it not be a
better thing to live together in
poverty? I cannot live and create in
the smug atmosphere, the righteousness,
of Denmark and your family. I will be
able to support you all, soon. But it
must be here, with me. I am sending
you a recent photograph of me, for each
of the children. I want them to
remember what I look like. Please
remind them that it is my birthday soon.
I should like to have a greeting. And
please speak French to them. I have
work to do. Have courage. Your
husband, Paul Gauguin.

(PAUL seals the letter in its
envelope, and rises. A pause.

He looks at VINCENT, makes a
decision, and puts the letter
down. He crosses to VINCENT, and
picks up VINCENT's sketchbook)

May I? (no response) There's nothing
in this book. What have you been doing
for the last three days? <u>Look</u>!

VINCENT: (sullenly) Nothing.

PAUL: Work. If neither of us can work, we'll
            go crazy. I'd rather leave.

VINCENT: If you leave, I won't be able to work.
            There are too many people counting on
            us to work together.

PAUL: That's why we can't paint.
            If an archer shoots for a prize of brass,
            his hand trembles.
            If he shoots for a prize of silver, his
            arm shakes.
            If he shoots for a prize of gold, he
            cannot see the target.
            If he shoots for nothing-- (gestures
            for "connects with target")

VINCENT: What about the School?

PAUL: If we don't paint...no School.

VINCENT: I cannot work like this. We have to
            work together or I don't work at all.

PAUL: Vincent--

VINCENT: We're giving up too early.

PAUL: I can't paint in these conditions. I
            have to work my way, too. Maybe I

should go back to Britanny. You're a
good painter, Vincent, but maybe you
should work alone... Maybe I'm holding
you back.

VINCENT: Yes, I _am_ a good painter. And I have a
way of working. After months of
painting _alone_ -- years! I may be too
rigid, I know that. But I _know_ we can
paint a common style. I know how to do
it!

PAUL: (firmly) Vincent, too often you want
to work your way, too often. We've
tried working side by side. We can't
create like that... The sun is shining.
We have a good day. Let's go outside.
Let's work on a subject in common
without helping each other. When we're
finished, we'll see what we have.

VINCENT: (rising) If we work together--

PAUL: I want to paint first, talk later.

VINCENT: All right. That's how we work.

PAUL: All right.

(They prepare to go out to paint,
fetching supplies and outdoor
clothing. PAUL dismantles the
VINCENT scarecrow to free
VINCENT's coat. They keep an
efficient distance from each
other as they speak)

You choose the subject.

VINCENT: The barracks.

PAUL: Too far.

VINCENT: The bridge over the river.

PAUL: Been there before.

VINCENT: The asylum. The fields to the south!

PAUL: The vineyards?

VINCENT: The vineyards.

> (PAUL steps directly and
> immediately into the scene of
> their painting, followed by
> VINCENT, who sputters in
> exasperation. PAUL is at his
> painting. VINCENT, frustrated
> with the task at hand, leaves
> his own canvas and compares it to
> PAUL's. He hovers behind PAUL's
> shoulders in agitation, yet
> holds off from speaking. PAUL
> finally, in frustration, speaks)

PAUL: What.

VINCENT: I need your help.

PAUL: We agreed to work apart, each for
            ourselves. No talking until we finish
            painting.

> (VINCENT backs off and keeps his
> silence. Finally, he is unable
> to control himself)

VINCENT: I can't get this. Those two figures.
            They look the same, only one is further
            back. When I put the lines down the
            same on the canvas, there's no depth!

> And those hills roll, yet they're part
> of the vineyard. How can I make that
> clear and <u>not</u> change the colour??

PAUL: You ask the wrong questions.

VINCENT: <u>What do I do</u>?!

PAUL: (in dismissal, but as a joke) Scrape
it off and start over.

> VINCENT stares at his canvas.
> PAUL resumes work. VINCENT
> starts scraping his canvas.
> PAUL looks at him incredulously,
> then packs and leaves abruptly.
> Lights fade.

Act Two, Scene Two

PAUL ALONE: AN INTERIOR
MONOLOGUE

> Moments later, PAUL comes into
> the house, carrying his partly
> finished canvas. He props it to
> one side, throws down his gear.
> Grabbing a bottle of wine, he
> pours a drink and tosses it back.
> He slumps in a chair, takes in
> the room.

What am I doing here?
A fish out of water in Arles.
Everything -- landscape, people--
seems small,   mean,   shabby.

I want
I want

            aaaahhh

to desire is a suffering
I want
        to paint
I can't paint
I am afraid   afraid

    If I should be doomed
        to never paint again
            to lose   this   now
If I should be so doomed
        to paint
                never   again

Forty
I'm forty
                how much left
My God
My God

I should be recognized by now

should have made it   by now

If I should be so doomed
    to paint
                never   again
I
who am empty-hearted
    without that
loving neither
                wife

                nor

                child
        is
            this
                criminal?

My father died
at sea
on our journey to Peru.
                        I was four
My mother died
whilst I was at sea
I was in India.
                        I was eighteen

                        I am forty.

I am afraid now

                      never

                              to know love

                              to know being loved

                                        again.

It was a crime

    for me to become a painter

I

am a criminal

          an outlaw

God

    I want

         I want

         not that

         please

God damn.

I have known

         yes

    the direst, the deepest poverty

I

mean

hunger

         and all the rest of it.

It is nothing.

         Or almost nothing.

One gets used to it.

One can laugh it off.   In the end

But the terrible thing is the way it
  prevents

you from working   yes   spending

your time   your energy   worrying

chasing after money

Suffering

Artists must suffer.

Too much suffering kills you.

    To desire desire

              is a suffering.

God damn.

I can't work

        but

God

    an artist is always an artist

    at the age of ten, of twenty, of one
      hundred--

    but isn't he better at some times

    than at others? Isn't he a living

    ordinary   human being?

God

God

God

        my wife

        my children

          Aline

                              please
                I want you
                I want
                              to paint

Well

O Gauguin
Where is
        your
        savage man
                    now?

Well,
this savage man
                    is closing
                    his heart.

I'm getting out.
Theo.

I'm getting out.

If I'm going to be a criminal
    I'll be a great criminal.

If I'm giving <u>that</u> up,   then I won't
waste my time spending it here.

No more backward steps
I've lost enough sight

No   No   No

Vincent

gets

no more blood

from this heart.

Act Two, Scene Three

FALLING APART

PAUL is alone in the Yellow
House, completing his letter
to Theo. VINCENT bursts in
with his completed canvas,
sets it down, rummages for
more supplies. He is unaware
of all else.

VINCENT: What are you doing?

PAUL: Writing a letter.

VINCENT: (enthusiastic) I need a different set
           of colours. More ochre. Prussian blue.
           Vermilion. Citron. Two knives. A
           harder brush... You were right. I was
           asking the wrong questions. I was only
           showing work when-- It was in scraping
           the canvas that--! I was working the
           canvas, working the same colours -- my
           arm -- I was working with my arms! As

they were. I had forgotten to work!
You can't paint something separate from
yourself. You were right!

PAUL: Vincent...?

VINCENT: I'm going back. Try it again!

PAUL: Vincent, we made an agreement. We
            weren't to speak to one another until
            the work was done. I wonder if you
            can hold to any agreement. You always
            want me to involve myself in your
            painting.

VINCENT: Yes, you have to be. And I have to be
            part of your paintings. That's how we
            work together. That's how we learn, to
            teach the others.

PAUL: You are not a part of my painting!

VINCENT: (after a pause to find the right words)
            Paul, when you told me to scrape that
            canvas, you saw what I was trying to
            paint. The colours I used were too
            stark... But when the paint mixed in
            the scraping, I made, I saw a new ground
            of colours -- colours existing in what I
            saw before me, but hadn't seen before.
            You were right! You gave this to me!
            The canvas is the palette!

PAUL: Vincent, it was a joke. I didn't see
            anything, didn't mean anything.

VINCENT: It doesn't matter how we found it. We
            found something today! A turning point.
            Now we can write Theo for the money to
            bring the others down here.

PAUL: It's not time yet. Why don't you go
            back to your painting.

VINCENT: No, it _is_ time. We have it now. The
            beginning of the School. We have to
            bring the others in. Show them what
            we've unlocked. We've found the key.

PAUL: Vincent... There is no key. I was
            joking. Telling you to scrape the
            canvas was a joke. You listen to the
            wrong things. You don't understand.
            You took me seriously... We can't
            work together. I'm going away. (takes
            up letter) I've written Theo and told
            him we can't work together.

VINCENT: You can't do that! He's _my_ brother.
            You can't write my brother without
            telling _me_!

PAUL: (rises) I did. Don't you ever listen?

VINCENT: You can't leave! Give me that letter.
            (reaches for letter)

PAUL: Do not touch me.

VINCENT: You are not sending that letter!!

            (VINCENT grabs for the letter.
            PAUL pushes him back, sending
            VINCENT sprawling on the floor)

PAUL: Back off before I kill you.

            (PAUL turns away in anger and
            speaks while leaving the house)

            I'm getting out!... I'm getting out.

VINCENT: This is _mine_!! This! is! _mine_!!

<u>Act Two, Scene Four</u>

VINCENT ALONE: AN INTERIOR
                 MONOLOGUE

VINCENT, collapsed on the floor,
is discovered to be in intense
interior prayer. He rises
slowly to his knees, eyes
closed, murmuring. Still
kneeling, his body relaxes.
Slowly, his eyes open. Almost
inaudibly, he completes the
meditation.

"I live now

            Not I

but Christ   lives in me"

I am   a new man

      I am   forgiven

I am

finally   where

            I was meant to be

        Paul   and I

        are opening the way

                and we

                will create

a painting that sells

Theo

this meagre

allowance of yours

transformed

into the

riches

of a corporation

the loaves and fishes

of the new age!

Cities

breed corruption

callousness

avarice

artist   turned against

artist

It is

Satan

who sits amongst us

pours the absinthe

sells the paintings

We must be

a monastery

a holy order

living in exile

out

under

this good sun

Our twelve chairs

will soon be filled

with

Brother Artists

We will

bring forth

a Baptistry of Light

send it North

show them

with these hands

eyes

heart

Food

and good health

and able   to work

work well!

as long

as God

wills it

And when

the work   is done

the School founded

then

I will

stop

painting

I will sit

in the sun

    a long red beard

    no!

    white

<u>old</u>!

    and healthy

And I will have

the young ones

    all around me

       with new light

       new colours

          in their hearts

    And they will ask me

    how it was

       in the beginning

What was Paul like?

    How was it

       when we both painted

Who learned what from whom?

    And Paris?

         when the new work

        was revealed

    I'll be

    the only one left

    They'll believe

whatever
I tell them
(laughs)
The Old Man
Old Grandpa

Do your work
my children
you are
my real kin
on this earth
And when Death comes
it will be
a Good Death
in the full light
of the midday
surrounded by my Family
all working
all painting
in the sun
all
in a
State
of Grace

Act Two, Scene Five

MADMEN

> Later that night. VINCENT is
> still on his knees in silent
> prayer. PAUL enters, smoking
> his pipe. He observes VINCENT
> silently, then makes a sound
> of disbelief and condescension.
> He hangs up his coat and
> begins to pack. VINCENT, only
> too aware of PAUL's presence,
> carefully rises, hangs up his
> coat, moves to sit at the table
> with a cup of wine. PAUL
> finds, amongst the baggage, his
> fencing foil, and brandishes
> it for effect.

PAUL: Have you ever fought before? Have you
           ever tried to kill someone? If you
           have to fight someone with a sword,
           someone who has fought before, take
           care. He is dangerous. He uses a
           sword as simply as he would a stick.
           Do not hesitate. Make the counter.
           And a quick blow on the head or in the
           face will settle him for you.

               (PAUL attacks VINCENT in jest)

VINCENT: Stop it. Leave me alone!

PAUL: Vincent, I'm making a man of you.

VINCENT: I'm man enough. I was a preacher in the
           mines when you were still a stockbroker.

I starved. I worked myself to
exhaustion. But I saved lives while
you were saving money.

PAUL: I quit that life. But I wasn't forced
out. I chose to paint.

VINCENT: The Church dismissed me because I spoke
the truth. I shamed them by living
with the miners. By living the example
of Christ.

PAUL: If Christ were a painter, He couldn't
sell anything. What good is a
sanctified failure?

VINCENT: You think in pieces of silver. I paint.
That's my sole purpose in being.

PAUL: Don't preach at me. I'll sell anything
and everything I can to keep going.
I'll make a living of this. Long before
you.

VINCENT: Go ahead. Support yourself. And your
family.

PAUL: My family is my business.

VINCENT: Then don't make it ours, mine and Theo's.
Why should we support you?

PAUL: That isn't charity. That's business,
between Theo and myself. You're out
of it.

VINCENT: You deserted them. That's the sin of
pride and self-service. I would give
anything to honour my life with a
family.

PAUL: Your record of honour so far is a few
months with a whore in The Hague.
Hoping to bless her litter with your
name. Except that she wouldn't keep
you.

VINCENT: She was a woman who tried to deal
honestly with the life that God gave
her to endure. Her soul was beautiful.
I drove her away. I was too demanding.
There was no money.

PAUL: The whore used you. You were convenient.
Just as Mette used me. She needed a
baby-making machine. But I love them.
Far more than she ever could.

VINCENT: But you're not there. She is. Someday
they'll forget you. Turn against you.

PAUL: I'm working. To be a success again.
But in my real vocation. Then they'll
come to me.

VINCENT: You think it will be so easy? I'm more
honest about it. I was told to leave
my family home. I have no wife. No
family of my own. But I don't hurt
anyone. I don't take anything away.
My paintings are my children. And I
give them everything.

PAUL: These aren't children. This is canvas.
Wood. Paint. I have children. My own
blood. You don't know what that means.

VINCENT: Every one of these is part of me.

PAUL: Is that so? (takes up VINCENT's
painting of "Madame Ginoux") What about
this? I call this "child" a bastard.
A copy from my painting!

VINCENT: (grabbing for painting, taking it)
            That's mine!

PAUL: Vincent van Gogh, stealing my painting!
            You're a thief. No! A "kidnapper."

VINCENT: I'm no thief, I copy to learn. You're
            the master, the great teacher -- it
            should fatten your massive ego. I
            borrow -- but you steal. Look at that
            canvas!

                    (VINCENT indicates PAUL's
                    painting on the wall, "Madame
                    Ginoux in the All-night Café")

PAUL: Yes, look at her. Madame Ginoux runs a
            café, she's almost illiterate. But you
            show her with a book -- the Good Book
            -- like some Muse.

VINCENT: It's a picture of her inner self, her
            spirit--!

PAUL: She's a lousy innkeeper -- "The Madonna
            of Absinthe"-- That's the truth, and
            my painting shows it.

VINCENT: It's a fraud! She runs a reputable
            hotel--

PAUL: Arles is one big prison. All the cells
            are the same.

VINCENT: Yours is a parody of my painting!!

                    (Incensed, VINCENT grabs his "All-
                    night Café" and virtually throws
                    it at PAUL)

Look at that background! Even the
colours are the same! (going to PAUL's
canvas) And don't think I don't see
him -- Papa Roulin, drunk at table.
Is that to belittle me? I think so.
My only two friends in this miserable
place and you show them in ruin...
(moving in on PAUL at the table) You
mock me. You pervert everything...
Fantastical colours. Rearranging the
landscape. Theo expects paintings of
Provence! -- not hallucinations!!

PAUL: You don't paint what's here. You paint
            Bible stories. The noble toil of
            farm-women. God's grace in a harvest.
            Slop! Millet is dead. Romanticism
            is dead!

VINCENT: Father Millet, in one canvas, teaches
            more about painting than you will ever
            know in a lifetime.

PAUL: Stop preaching, Captain, and paint.
            An arrangement of shapes and colours
            on a flat surface. Paint!!

VINCENT: Painting is the Word of God. You
            distort, you blaspheme. Theo will
            come here some day and he'll see your
            lies.

PAUL: (rises) Theo will punish Paul, punish
            Vincent. Grow up! Stop using Theo as
            a crutch. Writing him every day like
            a lovesick wife.

VINCENT: Theo gave me my life.

PAUL: Then he'll take it too. When he
            marries.

VINCENT: (pauses in shock, mumbles) ...Engaged.

PAUL: Theo is <u>marrying</u> Johanna. In the
            spring.

VINCENT: He won't, he <u>can't</u>...!

PAUL: I know. I saw the letter.

VINCENT: You're spying on me!!

> (PAUL now begins a relentless,
> though controlled, attack on
> VINCENT, backing him into a far
> corner)

PAUL: Give it a year. Two at the most. As
            soon as they have children, you're out
            in the cold. Just like me. Then you
            can start supporting yourself for the
            first time in your life. No more free
            time to paint parables and write
            beautiful letters. Just work. Like
            everyone else. Look at me. I don't
            whine and whimper. I've had malaria
            for a year but I don't complain. I
            just fight to stay alive. I work when
            I can. I have a job to do. (laughs)
            You can't do it on your own. You're a
            cripple. You hate, you stifle, you
            covet, you eat my blood. But I have
            no more to give. And neither does
            Theo. It's over. No school. No
            painting. Nothing.

> (VINCENT is completely stunned,
> withdrawn. PAUL walks away, sits
> in his chair at the table. There
> is nothing more to say. Long
> pause. Finally, VINCENT turns,

                    (a piece of charcoal in his hand,
                    and walks with purpose to the
                    area in front of PAUL, kneels.
                    On the floor, he stares, then
                    scrawls quickly. He sits back,
                    reads the message, slowly)

VINCENT: "I am the Holy Spirit. I am whole in
            spirit."

                    (He looks to PAUL, who has been
                    drawn in, but guardedly.
                    VINCENT is triumphant, but PAUL
                    maintains a blank expression.
                    VINCENT panics, turns back to the
                    scrawl, tracing it out with his
                    finger, as if it is seeping away
                    into the floorboards)

            I am -- the -- Holy -- Spirit! I.
            Am. Whole. In spirit!

                    (PAUL registers the state of
                    affairs, which includes himself
                    trapped still in the house. Then
                    he closes himself off. VINCENT
                    scrabbles at the floor with his
                    nails, falling forward over the
                    scrawl)

            I am the Holy Spirit!! I am...whole...
            in...spirit... (fades in a whimper)

                    Fade to black. Pause.

Act Two, Scene Six

PACKING UP

> The following morning. PAUL is
> finishing packing. VINCENT
> watches him uneasily.

VINCENT: The train is only five hours away.
There are too many canvases to crate
before then...I could send them on to
you later.

PAUL: All right.

VINCENT: Where should I send them?

PAUL: I don't know yet. I'll send the address
to you.

VINCENT: (bringing over something) Here...it
was in the corner.

> (VINCENT pours a cup of coffee,
> hands it to PAUL)

Coffee.

PAUL: Oh.

> (PAUL doesn't take it. VINCENT
> puts it on the table)

VINCENT: Boots -- I forgot the boots! I have
these boots Theo sent me. They're too
large for me... (finds them) But you
could wear them. I have these anyway.
You need new boots. Winter is coming...
Try them on...

(PAUL takes the boots, but does
not try them on. VINCENT finds
a rag, moves to scrub the
charcoal off the floorboards.
PAUL watches him)

It's the wind here that makes the
winter so bad... I should rebuild the
shutters on the windows upstairs.
Roulin could help... I've already done
his portrait, but I haven't done his
wife or family... That's enough work
to last inside the winter... When the
sun comes back I'm going to work more
slowly. I've been pushing too hard...
(stops scrubbing) Do they fit?

PAUL: Yes...they're fine... You should use
            the winter to restore yourself.

VINCENT: Yes, I have to work all the time...

PAUL: No. You should rest. Don't push the
            painting. You should try to get in
            one good shit a day, get plenty of
            rest, go to the whorehouse once a
            week. And eat twice a day.

VINCENT: You're right...I think I could change.
            It would be the most difficult thing
            I've ever done. I'm sorry all this
            has happened. I wish I'd known two
            months ago-- You need some breakfast.
            You shouldn't travel on an empty
            stomach, with the trouble it's been
            giving you... I'll cook some eggs--

                (PAUL crosses to VINCENT, takes
                VINCENT's head in both hands and
                looks deeply into his eyes)

Paul??

>   (PAUL releases VINCENT and takes
>   up the letter)

PAUL: Here. My letter to Theo. Tear it up.

>   VINCENT takes it and does this
>   happily. PAUL's response is
>   mixed. Fade to black.

Act Two, Scene Seven

ALL-NIGHT DRUNK

>   Very late at night. PAUL and
>   VINCENT are drinking wine and
>   absinthe at the table. PAUL
>   carves a small wooden panel,
>   VINCENT sketches.

PAUL: I don't like living like this. You know
what they were going to do at my
brokerage house? I was making thirty
thousand francs a year. They were
going to fire me. So I quit. Most of
those people didn't even know I painted.
I thought I could survive by painting.
For three years now, I've promised
Mette that I would be able to support
her and the children -- any day. I
was wrong.

VINCENT: Sometimes I think it's not our work
           that fails -- it's you and me. Look
           at Manet, Renoir -- they're making a
           living...

PAUL: What are they doing now? The same
           thing over and over.

VINCENT: It's almost working for us, it's
           almost good enough...

PAUL: The paintings, yes, the paintings are
           good... If people saw a great artist
           walking down the street they'd kill
           him. What we need is a secret society
           to protect ourselves. We would all
           wear tattered and worn clothing.
           Cloaks and cowls to hide our faces.
           We would have passwords. And of course,
           a secret handshake. That way, artists
           could keep in touch with each other
           without anyone else knowing. A secret
           society. Like the Masons. We might
           be starving but at least we'd know
           each other. The Great Artists...

VINCENT: A Brotherhood of Artists.

               (PAUL loses interest, returns to
                his carving. VINCENT pursues
                his line of thought)

           A brotherhood sharing in holy work,
           sharing one work. An order of monks
           making one great painting... We could.
           A new kind of art! My brush strokes,
           your colours... Bernard, the outlines.
           Lautrec does the figures, with Degas
           arranging them on the canvas. Seurat...
           well, he mixes all the pigments. The

animals and plants belong to Rousseau!
Cezanne, the apples...apples and...?

(Defeated by the growing complexity
of the scheme, VINCENT turns to
PAUL)

What are you carving?

PAUL: This is the moon. This is the woman.
And this is her great cunt. And this
is the fox down here. Turning into a
hand. Reaching up to grab her, pull
her down into the ocean.

VINCENT: The Devil...you let the Devil into your
work.

PAUL: Where's the Devil, Vincent?

VINCENT: The Devil's inside. God is outside, in
the world. We go outside to paint God's
Word.

PAUL: God's inside. The Devil's outside.
Decay and death. You should know that.
You're the preacher.

VINCENT: Not a preacher, no hypocrite. A true
man of God. A worker.

PAUL: What's a worker? How can you call
yourself a worker?

VINCENT: My hair is falling out. My teeth are
rotting. Look at these clothes! My
hands -- they're torn...

PAUL: What's a worker? It's not in your hands.
Your clothes. Your body. What is it?

VINCENT: (finding the image) A worker is someone who manifests God in the world.

PAUL: Manifests God? A worker is someone who makes things. A man makes bread. Shoes. A table.

VINCENT: I create with paint the way God creates with flesh.

PAUL: So. You're God.

VINCENT: I'm not God.

PAUL: Then why do you have twelve chairs in this yellow house when there's only two of us? What does that make Theo -- Saint Peter? I think I don't like your brother.

VINCENT: He's saved you...

PAUL: He lives off me. He lives off you. I send him the paintings. He sells them. But I don't have to like him. We're whores. And what does that make Theo?

VINCENT: I won't let you say that...

PAUL: We're bad whores. We almost give it away. My whore is bad -- gives it to me for nothing. Your whore is a good whore -- makes you pay. We're not even good whores... Ahh, here I've been carving all night and you've been feeling sorry for yourself and your pimp brother. Vincent, you don't fuck enough. Why don't you go out and get fucked?

VINCENT: (rises) If it weren't for Theo, you'd still be sick in bed in Britanny. Theo works <u>with</u> us. He does half our work. You should put his name on your paintings right beside your own!

> (VINCENT scrawls with his charcoal on PAUL's carving. PAUL pushes away from the table, lurches to his feet, grabs his knife. VINCENT, startled, starts to move away, trips, falls to the floor. PAUL hurls sketch paper at VINCENT)

PAUL: Take that paper, "worker," and manifest God!

> (PAUL backs VINCENT into a corner with his knife)

Where's God, Vincent? You're the preacher! Don't you know?

VINCENT: Can't tell you.

PAUL: Draw God!

> (VINCENT cowers, drawing a curving V-shape on the sheet of paper. The devil's horns? His initial?)

What's that...? A woman's ass? Oh. A crow. <u>Caaaawwww</u>!!

VINCENT: Evil...you're <u>evil</u>!

PAUL: "I am the black holy spirit. I am the wholly black spirit."

(VINCENT is terrified)

Caw! Caw. This is a very good drawing, Vincent. I never could have drawn that. See. I've taught you to draw God. Aren't you going to thank me? Say thank you daddy teacher. Go on. Spit it out. Say thank you daddy teacher... Go on, say it... Thank you daddy teacher...

(PAUL repeats this ad lib. with increasing viciousness. Finally, defiant yet terrified, VINCENT speaks)

VINCENT: Thank you!!

(VINCENT collapses. PAUL forgets his intent and ambles away)

PAUL: Let's go to the whorehouse... C'mon, let's go to the whorehouse. I'll pay your way tonight. It's the last of the money anyway...

(VINCENT is frozen)

Cccccccaaaaaaaaaaaaaaaaaaaawwwwwww!!!

VINCENT shrinks. PAUL turns away. Blackout.

Act Two, Scene Eight

BREAKTHROUGH

PAUL and VINCENT, isolated,
though they appear to be in
the Yellow House, send word
to the outside.

PAUL:

VINCENT:

Dear Theo,
I think at this time
our friend Gauguin
is out of sorts
with this town of Arles,
and especially
with me.

Oh my friend,
if you could only
see me now. Vincent,
I'm afraid,
is at an impasse.

He has told me
he wishes to go
but has not reached
a definite decision as yet.

So I'm going
to go away.

Either he will definitely
go

Drives me crazy.

or he will definitely stay.

I'm going to Paris.
Two or three days.
Speak to Theo van Gogh.
So I will see you soon.
Please do not make
mention
of this letter
to anyone.

I shall write you in
two or three days

as soon as he makes this
decision.

We haven't done a piece
of work in two weeks.

We've been stuck
inside the house all
this time.

It is a pity
Vincent has this bad
sickness. Perhaps one
day he will overcome
it. I can't hold a
grudge against an
excellent heart
that is ill,
and suffering.

Despite his problems

he is a great painter,

and has a kind heart.

(pause)

Vincent   Vincent
Vincent   Vincent
oh
Vincent

Despite this conflict,
the work goes well.

The wind has not stopped
us from going out to
paint.

Our discussions have
been terribly electric.

Paul is a man who knows
his own mind.
Every painter finds
what he must have,
and we must respect him.

In haste,

A handshake,

Vincent

(pause)

I'm sorry   I'm sorry
I'm sorry   I'm sorry
I'm sorry   I'm sorry
I'm sorry   I'm sorry

Well

                    a lie

Well

                    a lie

Here I am

VINCENT: This is a lie. It's a lie! Vincent. My _name_. Not a lie. _I'm_ Vincent. Vincent is not dead. A dead brother. _Vincent_ died. Father died. A house of women. Women, and fragile men. (now fighting his hallucinatory voices) Alone. Leave me alone!

PAUL: Done _nothing_ since I've come here.

VINCENT: I'll paint you... Yes, I'll paint your portrait. (now overlapping with PAUL) No, I'll paint you. Yes, I'll see you. I can see you!! See you!!

PAUL: (overlaps with VINCENT above) Need to do _something_. I'll do an exercise. I'll paint exactly what I see. Paint what's in front of me. No one will believe you, Gauguin!

        (PAUL laughs. He grabs his painting gear, rushes to the outdoor area. Simultaneously VINCENT clears away space in the house to work on a canvas Neither has awareness of the other as they move to set up. PAUL is quickly set up. He concentrates on the scene before him. VINCENT, as he completes his preparation, lastly finds

(the torn shreds of PAUL's letter
to Theo. He stares at the
fragments, then plays with them,
lets them flutter to the floor,
watches them land)

PAUL: VINCENT:

Snow. Trees. Garden.
Snow.
Nothing in the heart.
Can't see anything.
Paint what I see.   Flowers... Garden...
Before me.   Women in a garden!
Paint what you see   We won't go out.
before you.   I can paint you
Paint.   inside,
Paint what's real.   inside the house,
                               inside
                               my head.
                               Paint
Marks in the dead space.   the inside of my head!
Make them live.   Paint
Paint like a child.   just like you want to
                               see it.
                               as innocently
                               as a child.

Nothing happened yet.

Ah. I see.
Take them out.
Put them back.   Just a story.
                               How it might have been.

Gauguin,
paint what's real.
Red fence. All right.
                               A child...
White road.   I'm a child.
Ahh roses.   A real child.
Only what's there, Paul.   Child Vincent.

94

Only what's there.

I can put the women on a
path,
path in the garden.
Put Mother here --
but it's not her --
It's me!
and I can be whatever I
want.
Garden.
Path. Women.

Two women.
Catch them quick.
Camera. Before they go.
There.
Got them.

See.
Haven't got them
yet.
There. In the centre.

It's all right.
Garden is only
on the canvas...
Faces will stay where
I put them.

(laughs)
Amber. Yellow.
And this is chrome.
Two women.
Don't move.

(a discovery)
That's what he meant!
Why I can change things.
I can change things.
That's me.

Hand over mouth.
Bet she has a toothache.

Every painting is a
portrait of me.
That's also me, on a
little walk here in the
field,
sister in the field.
If I want a sun? --
the whole canvas is sun!
the canvas -- the women --

There, shore.
Green grass.
Blue.
Blue.
Only what's there, Paul

There's a face in the
bush.
Who'd believe you, Paul?
There's a face in the
bush!

(laughs)
It's a joke!!
It's a joke!!

light--
Listen to the light.
When I paint them,
I don't hear them.
When I see them
I can't hear them!
Change them!

I _can_ change!

I can change Vincent!!

(Both canvases, which we have not
seen as yet, are completed as
one. PAUL rushes into the house,
finds VINCENT just propping up
his painting, in a state of
exhaltation. The audience is
the first to see the twin
canvases, at first glance
disturbingly similar; they are
adaptations of PAUL's "Women of
Arles in the Asylum Garden" and
VINCENT's "Memories of the Garden
at Etten." VINCENT is absorbed,
PAUL exuberant. PAUL, laughing,
holds out his canvas for VINCENT)

PAUL: Look! That's what was there!

(VINCENT recoils in shock. PAUL
puts it down, crosses to VINCENT's
painting)

Let's see. What do you have? (sees
it) That's what was there! (excited,

and as a joke) You stole my painting!!

VINCENT: (clutching it to himself) Shut up!

PAUL: It's even my style.

VINCENT: (pulling away) You can't see it. You can't have it. My self...me...

PAUL: No. You painted it. It's very good.

VINCENT: You -- told me what to paint. What to see!

PAUL: Now we come together. Now we come together!

VINCENT: (overlapping) I'm supposed to do it, I'm supposed to do it! Not you. Not you!

PAUL: (coldly) You have to do it all, don't you, Dutchman.

VINCENT: You're taking this from me! Why are you taking this from me??

PAUL: We did it! The first one. Every day we do that...

VINCENT: How can we see the same thing? Paint the same thing?!

PAUL: I don't know, but we did.

            (VINCENT pushes the canvas out of his own hands. PAUL is drawn to it)

Very full of God. Martha and Mary.

Sisters of Jesus. Women from the tomb.
Very full of God--

VINCENT: (overlapping) Sisters of Jesus -- are
going to the tomb. Sisters of Jesus
are going to the tomb. Sisters of
Jesus -- that's not the tomb.
(crossing to PAUL's canvas) That's
the asylum!

PAUL: I painted what I saw.

VINCENT: (turning on him) Why did you stop
there?

PAUL: I stop where my heart opens.

VINCENT: (riding him) The asylum -- why
there?

PAUL: What did you paint?

VINCENT: (almost to himself) I don't know any
more...

PAUL: It doesn't matter--

VINCENT: (sudden snarl) I have to know what I
paint!!

PAUL: (simply) That's what you paint.

VINCENT: (spitting) It's ugly!!

PAUL: (turns away coldly) You turn
everything to shit.

VINCENT: (following PAUL) You're not here.

PAUL: Go for a walk! (trying to keep control)

VINCENT: (closely, over his shoulder) You go,
Paul, <u>you</u> go. (hissing) Judas.
Judassssss! <u>Judassss</u>!!

          VINCENT flees the house.
          Blackout.

          <u>Act Two, Scene Nine</u>

          THE END

          Later that night.

          PAUL is discovered in the
          house, pouring absinthe. He
          sits alone at the table. He
          is drunk. He drinks, fiddles
          with a carving.

          VINCENT comes into the doorway,
          in a stupor. He stares at
          PAUL, the room, the lamp above
          the table. He moves slowly to
          the table, as PAUL simply stops
          moving, waits. VINCENT takes
          up PAUL's glass of absinthe,
          moves away, his back to PAUL.
          VINCENT looks into the glass,
          takes a small sip. A pause.

          Suddenly, VINCENT whirls around,
          pitches the contents of the

glass, with a slap, into
PAUL's face. PAUL leaps
angrily to his feet, roars,
makes as if to strike back.

VINCENT holds his ground, but
crumples, ready for the blow.
A moment of recognition.

PAUL relaxes, goes to VINCENT.
PAUL takes VINCENT into his
arms, and lays him down, a
rigid Pietà.

VINCENT lies on the floor, a
series of small shakes and
seizures running through his
body.

PAUL stands over him for a
moment, moves as if to leave,
puts on his coat, pauses.
Then he returns to the table,
sits, and slumps into a heavy
sleep.

The lights fade to deep night:
shadows and silhouette.

A pause. PAUL awakens to find
VINCENT standing over him,
silent, staring intently as
in a trance. PAUL does not
rise, merely looks at VINCENT.
He speaks quietly.

PAUL: What are you doing, Vincent?

             (VINCENT makes no response. He
             continues to stare, then abruptly

                    not moved during this sequence,
                    turns and addresses the audience.
                    Instead of running away, VINCENT
                    collapses onto the ground)

PAUL: That night I stayed in a hotel. The
                    next morning, Christmas Eve, Vincent
                    was discovered, unconscious, in the
                    yellow house. He had lost a lot of
                    blood. I sent a telegram to Theo. He
                    came, and put Vincent in a hospital.
                    Theo and I left for Paris together,
                    after Christmas. I never saw Vincent
                    again.

                    (PAUL walks to the isolated
                    corner from where he began the
                    play. VINCENT has let the
                    razor occupy his clenched fist,
                    examining it intensely yet
                    dispassionately. He looks past
                    it, lets it slide away in his
                    hand, onto the ground)

                    I have to leave Europe. I've gone to
                    Martinique. I've gone to America.
                    Have to go even further. A terrible
                    epoch is being prepared for the
                    coming generation. The reign of gold.

                    (VINCENT now fixes his attention
                    on something warm and growing in
                    the air beyond him, draws up
                    slightly towards it, lets it
                    work on him)

                    In my dream, an angel with white wings
                    came to me, smiling; behind him, an old
                    man. The angel said: "Ask the old man

to lead you to Infinity. You will see
what God wants to do with you and you
will feel that today you are remarkably
incomplete. For what would the
Creator's work be if it were done in
a single day? God never rests."

The vision turns black, as
VINCENT's open hands contract
to fists, move to clench his
skull. Fade to black.

The End

> moves away, in a slow but
> purposeful walk. PAUL lays his
> head down to sleep, then
> discovers VINCENT standing over
> him a second time)

Vincent, what are you doing?

> (Again no response. VINCENT
> withdraws, approaches a third
> time)

PAUL: What are you doing?!

> (VINCENT registers an unreadable
> change, turns and goes. PAUL
> rises and moves purposefully
> from the table, towards the
> outdoors area. PAUL hears
> footsteps, turns sharply to face
> VINCENT, who runs up behind him
> with the straight-edge razor,
> open and poised to slash. PAUL
> holds his ground, fixes VINCENT
> with his eyes. VINCENT stops
> little more than an arm's length
> away, the razor clenched aloft.

They stand, their eyes locked.

Finally, VINCENT averts his eyes,
lowers the razor, and runs away.
VINCENT, now locked in a
repetitive phrase of movement,
attacks PAUL twice more, with
the identical rhythm and sequence
of motions. At the third attack,
when VINCENT averts his eyes and
lowers the razor, PAUL, who has

About the Authors:

DENNIS HAYES came to Canada in 1968 as a visiting professor, for a year. He stayed. After receiving a B.Sc. in Biology and Chemistry, he was a fellow in the Playwright's Workshop at State University of Iowa, 1957-58. He has pursued his development as a primary artist in theatre since then. In Canada he turned to non-representational theatre, exploring it intensively as actor, director, and playwright. Of particular value were the years spent as a student of Frau Til Thiele, and working with Judy Jarvis on techniques of bringing improvisation to theatre performance as jazz musicians bring it to their performances. His works since 1968 include: PASSION II, DEATH OF ARTAUD, PROPHET I & PROPHET II, SPACES, HOSTAGE and THE YELLOW HOUSE AT ARLES. Two works-in-progress, THE SHEPHERD KING OF DETROIT CITY and THE 'NAM, deal with the Vietnam experience.

RICHARD PAYNE is a Presentational Artist in art/ writing/theatre. His training includes a BFA in Painting with Lawren P. Harris, a B.Ed. in Dramatic Arts, and an MFA in Creative Writing with George McWhirter. He is a past Drama Editor of PRISM international, and for two years was a theatre/ writing instructor for the University of Victoria Programme in federal prisons. As a member of George Luscombe's Toronto Workshop Productions company (1973-76), he was a contributor to the internationally acclaimed TEN LOST YEARS. His first play, A GAME OF HATS (1969), was performed in the National Arts Centre Studio for the Canadian University Drama League Festival '70. He has since devised several Drama Education playscripts, including THE ASSASSINATION OF D'ARCY MCGEE (University of Toronto, 1972), METROPOLE (Ontario Arts Council Artists-in-the-Schools, 1977), and ALFRED JARRY'S CIRCUS LUDICROUS PRESENTS "BOSS UBU"